Pebble® Plus

Meet Desert ANIMALS

SCORPIONS

by Rose Davin

raintree
a Capstone company — publishers for children

Raintree is an imprint of Capstone Global Library Limited, a company incorporated in
England and Wales having its registered office at 264 Banbury Road, Oxford, OX2 7DY –
Registered company number: 6695582

www.raintree.co.uk
myorders@raintree.co.uk

ISBN 978 1 4747 3657 2
20 19 18 17 16
10 9 8 7 6 5 4 3 2 1

British Library Cataloguing in Publication Data
A full catalogue record for this book is available from the British Library.

Editorial Credits
Marysa Storm and Alesha Sullivan, editors; Kayla Rossow, designer;
Ruth Smith, media researcher; Kathy McColley, production specialist

Photo Credits
Alamy: © Nature Picture Library, 13; Capstone Press: 6; naturepl.com: Angelo Gandolfi,
21; Shutterstock: Againstar, 17, Asian Images, 2, 24, Audrey Snider-Bell, 11, Charly
Morlock, 1, Dennis W. Donohue, 9, 24, EcoPrint, 7, IanRedding, 5, Mikhail Egorov, cover,
optionm, 22; TopFoto: © Photoshot, 15; Visuals Unlimited: Fabio Pupin, 19

Note to Parents and Teachers

The Meet Desert Animals set supports national curriculum standards for science
related to life science and ecosystems. This book describes and illustrates scorpions.
The images support early readers in understanding the text. The repetition of words
and phrases helps early readers learn new words. This book also introduces early
readers to subject-specific vocabulary words, which are defined in the Glossary
section. Early readers may need assistance to read some words and to use the Table
of Contents, Glossary, Read more, Websites, Comprehension questions and Index
sections of the book.

Printed and bound in China.

CONTENTS

DESERT HUNTERS

At night scorpions creep out of their burrows. They sit quietly in the darkness until prey comes near. Then they grab their prey. Sting! It's a mouse for dinner!

scorpion in its burrow

Scorpions live on every continent except

Antarctica. Many live in deserts.

But some scorpions live in grasslands or forests.

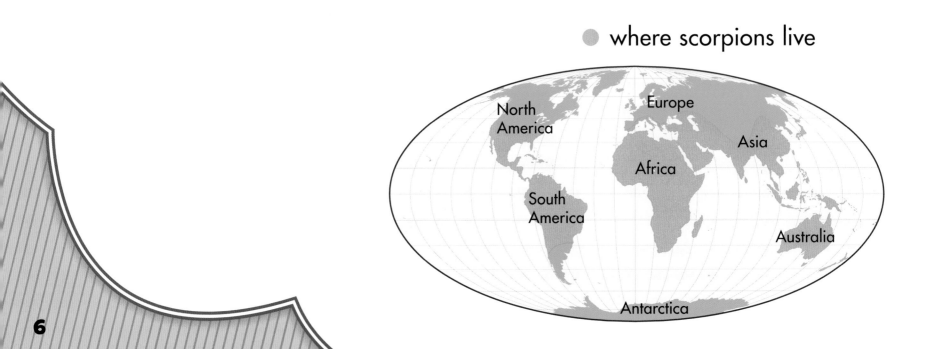

where scorpions live

North America

Europe

Asia

Africa

South America

Australia

Antarctica

6

PINCERS AND STINGERS

Desert scorpions are usually black,

brown or yellow. Most are about

8 centimetres (3 inches) long.

Some can be more than

18 centimetres (7 inches) long.

Scorpions are arachnids.

They have eight legs. Scorpions have

front pincers that are like claws.

They have stingers at the end of their tails.

stinger

pincer

leg

TIME TO EAT

Hungry scorpions grab prey when it comes close. They hold small prey with their pincers. Then they start eating.

Large, wiggling animals are harder
to eat. Scorpions raise their tail stinger.
Zap! The venom in the stinger
makes the animal unable to move.
It can also kill the animal.

LIFE CYCLE

Female scorpions give birth to 25 or more live young. They are all white. Newborns climb on their mothers' backs.

Newborns live on food already in their bodies. Later mothers kill prey for their young and leave it near them. Young scorpions stay near their mothers for two or three years.

Owls, lizards and snakes eat scorpions.
Scorpions use their stingers to
attack predators. Scorpions that stay safe
can live for about five years in the wild.

Glossary

arachnid small animal that has eight legs and two body sections; scorpions and spiders are arachnids

burrow tunnel or hole in the ground made or used by an animal

continent one of Earth's seven large land masses

creep move very slowly and quietly

desert area of dry land with few plants; deserts receive very little rain

pincer body part that is like a claw; scorpions use their pincers to catch prey

predator animal that hunts other animals for food

prey animal hunted by another animal for food

stinger long, sharp hollow body part; poison flows through the stinger into the prey

venom poison in an animal's stinger used to harm or kill another animal

Read more

Minibeasts, Spiders and Insects (Deadly Factbook), Steve Backshall (Franklin Watts, 2014)

Scorpion (A Day in the Life: Desert Animals), Anita Ganeri (Raintree, 2012)

Scorpion (Creepy Crawly Critters), Katie Marsico (Cherry Lake Publishing, 2015)

Websites

http://www.bbc.co.uk/nature/life/Scorpion

Discover facts and watch videos of scorpions on the BBC website.

http://animals.nationalgeographic.com/animals/bugs/scorpion/

Learn all about scorpions.

Comprehension questions

1. What body parts help scorpions get food?

2. Why do you think scorpions stay close to their mothers for two or three years?

Index